Practice Like The Pros

by Sue Terry

Discover the favorite practice routines of today's finest sax players.
Each artist gives you a personal look at how to practice
that can help you improve your technical ability
as you develop your own personal sound and style.
Included are exercises and tips relating to technique, tone and intonation,
musicianship, scales and chords, articulation, ear training, and much more.

Amsco Publications
New York/London/Paris/Sydney/Copenhagen/Madrid

ACKNOWLEDGEMENTS

Special Thanks to Peter Pickow, Sat Hon, Tim Price,
Wallace Collins, Derwyn Holder, Ed Lozano, Jerald Cole,
and especially to Gil Barretto, who got me from *mi* to *fa*.

More information on the players featured in this book can be found on the Internet at
www.sueterry.net/PLTP.

This book is dedicated to the memory of Thomas Chapin and Manny Boyd.

Photo Credits

page

6	Viv Stoll
7, 23	Elizabeth Lehman
8	Ray Block
10	Alejandra Freidman
12	© 1985 by Ronald Eckstein
14	Jerry Sheik
15	R. Andrew Lepley/New York
17	Lloyd Rucker
18	© Jeffery Kliman
20	Carol Goss
22	Arthur Elgort
25	Mark Vinci
26	Regine Romain
27	© Noah Greenberg 2001
29	Alfred Silvera
31	Peter Cook
34	Pierre DuFour
37	Fernando Natalici
38	© Nina D'Alessandro. All Rights Reserved

Cover photograph: SuperStock
Project editor: Peter Pickow
Interior design and layout: Len Vogler

Order No. AM 973808
US International Standard Book Number: 0.8256.1930.0
UK International Standard Book Number: 0.7119.9285.1

Exclusive Distributors:
Music Sales Corporation
257 Park Avenue South, New York, NY 10010 USA
Music Sales Limited
8/9 Frith Street, London W1D 3JB England
Music Sales Pty. Limited
120 Rothschild Street, Rosebery, Sydney, NSW 2018, Australia

Printed in the United States of America by
Vicks Lithograph and Printing Corporation

CONTENTS

CD CONTENTS

Disc 1

Introduction
Carol Chaikin ....Musicianship
Sheila Cooper........................Musicianship, Ear Training
Laura Dreyer.........................Scales, Patterns
Mark Friedman......................Improvisation
Samuel Furnace.....................Advanced Warmup, Intonation, Chord Study
Dave Glasser ....Articulation
Mark Gross............................Rhythm, Improvisation
Cleave Guyton ....Basic Warmup, Scale Study
Jenny Hill..............................Tone, Intonation
Martha Hyde ....Chord Study

Disc 2

Virginia Mayhew ....Basic Warmup, Scale Study
Andy Middleton.....................Patterns
Tom Murray ....Improvisation
Tom Olin ....Advanced Warmup, Chord Study
Jay Rodriguez........................Ear Training, Musicianship
Benny Russell ....Chord Study, Patterns
Andrew Sterman ....Breathing
Taimur Sullivan.....................Overtones
Jorge Sylvester.......................Ear Training, Patterns
Sue Terry ....Tone, Intonation

PREFACE

Dear Saxophonist,

All of us have had this experience at one time or another: We get ready to practice, then can't think of anything to play. Or else we know we should practice, but we feel uninspired. This book should remedy that problem—it's like getting a private lesson with twenty different teachers!

When I first began to approach my colleagues about contributing their knowledge to this collection of saxophone exercises, the response was overwhelming. Almost without exception, everyone I approached was eager to be a part of the book, and even more eager to practice out of it when it would be done.

My admiration toward my colleagues who appear in these pages is unbounded. They are the lifeblood of saxophone playing today. You hear them on the radio, on film soundtracks and CDs; you see them on television, film, video, in live concerts, and on Broadway. You hear them accompanying today's biggest stars. They are among the world's top professional players. Here is the inside scoop on what they have been practicing to get them where they are today.

My colleagues and I wish you much success in your playing. Keep practicing!

Note: Throughout this book, enharmonic equivalents are used for easier reading. For those of you seeking more detailed explanations of music theory and the musical terms used in this book, please consult *Theory and Harmony for the Contemporary Musician* by Arnie Berle.

CAROL CHAIKIN

Carol Chaikin has toured extensively throughout the U.S. as well as Europe, Japan, and Brazil, both as a leader and a sideperson. Her self-titled debut CD is on Gold Castle Records, and her latest project, Lucy's Day Off, is on Ms. Ecstasy Records. Ms. Chaikin has also recorded with Astrud Gilberto, DIVA, Unpredictable Nature, Mary Watkins, Maiden Voyage, Maria Anadon, Art Lillard, John Margolis, and Mark Lambert.

This is an exercise in accuracy, timing, and execution. It was passed on to me from the late and great Carmine Caruso. Take a difficult riff or written excerpt and decide on the ideal tempo you want to execute. Then cut the tempo exactly in half. If it is still difficult, cut it in half again. This enables your body to be in sync with your mind.

SHEILA COOPER

Sheila Cooper is a Canadian-born saxophonist, singer, and producer/arranger now living in Brooklyn, New York. She has performed and/or recorded with Nancy Wilson, Clark Terry, Renee Rosnes, Kenny Drew, Jr., Kenny Wheeler, Lewis Nash, Billy Drummond, Ed Howard, Lorne Lofsky, and Scott Colley. Ms. Cooper has been featured in several industrial films and TV commercials, and she was the onstage saxophonist in the Broadway production of Cabaret *with Joel Grey. Also an educator, she has taught at the Poysdorf Austria Jazz Workshop, the Innsbruck Jazz Workshop, and the Herne Musik Hochschuler Vocal Clinic. Her recording* Since You Were Mine *is on Panorama Records.*

I've found this exercise to be very helpful in developing the inner ear for instrumentalists as well as vocalists. It requires a smattering of piano competence.

Using any one of Bach's four-part chorales, play any three parts on the piano (or guitar) while singing the fourth part at the same time. Do this with all four parts, making adjustments as needed to suit the register of your voice; *e.g.*, women sing the bass part up the octave, men the soprano part down the octave (or in falsetto). The quality of your voice is irrelevant—just sing the correct notes as in-tune as you can.

Once you are able to sing the parts, repeat the exercise, but instead of singing the fourth part, imagine it inside your head while playing the other three parts. Strive to hear that fourth part internally, as clearly as the other three parts that you are playing externally.

Speed is not an issue.

LAURA DREYER

Laura Dreyer has been a professional saxophonist and flutist in New York City since 1982. She performs in diverse musical situations from bebop to Brazilian, and has been featured in the bands of Walter Bishop, Jr., Dom Salvador, DIVA, Nnenna Freelon, Dr. Billy Taylor, Helcio Milito, Mark Levine, and many others. She leads her own band, Mysterious Encounter, a Brazilian jazz quartet featuring her compositions and arrangements. Ms. Dreyer appears on recordings by Hendrik Meurkens, Rogerio Botter Maio, DIVA, and Fiveplay, as well as her own CD, Mysterious Encounter.

The following exercise is an adaptation of one that was suggested to me by Joe Viola when I was a student at Berklee College of Music. Make up a different pattern each day and try to play through all the major scales on the different degrees, ascending and descending, through the entire register of the horn. If you like to challenge yourself, there are many different ways to vary this concept, for example:
- apply a pattern to different arpeggios (major, minor, dominant, diminished)
- play a pattern chromatically
- play a pattern around a circle of 5ths
- play in an odd meter

The fun thing is that you get to use your creativity and develop your ear/hand connection, which is helpful for improvisation. It also greatly improves your ability to be fluent in all twelve keys.

C Major scale pattern starting with interval of a third
(To be played in all twelve keys)

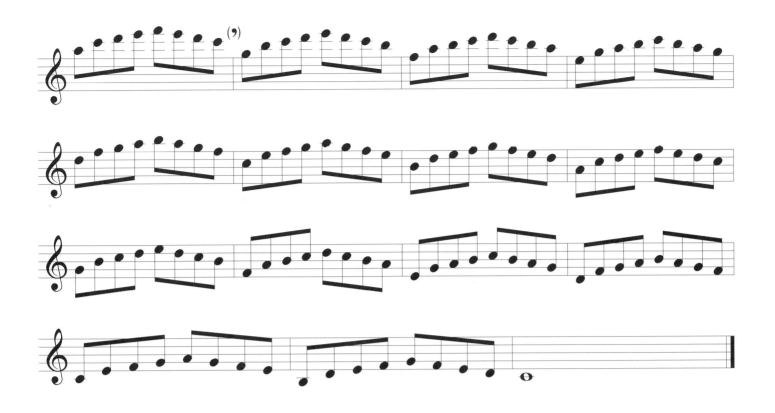

Other pattern examples

etc.

etc.

etc.

etc.

MARK FRIEDMAN

Mark Friedman has toured, performed, and recorded with Frank Sinatra, Buddy Rich, Tito Puente, Dizzy Gillespie, Manhattan Transfer, the Glenn Miller Band, the Four Tops, the Temptations, Frankie Valli, Andy Williams, Little Anthony, and numerous others, including a Grammy Award winning record with Machito. Currently he has many woodwind students in the New York metropolitan area. Mr. Friedman is on the adjunct music faculties of Ramapo High School and the Ridgewood Community School.

Many young jazz players are quick to run out of ideas. It is imperative to listen to the pros and legends of jazz to open one's ears and to take in as much of the vocabulary as possible. These licks are intended as a springboard to aid the improviser in developing his or her own improvisation skills. The II V(b9) I progressions incorporate the sound of the diminished scale and chord on the dominant chord. They are written in the key of G and are analyzed note-by-note for each chord. This will help you in transposing these examples to other keys.

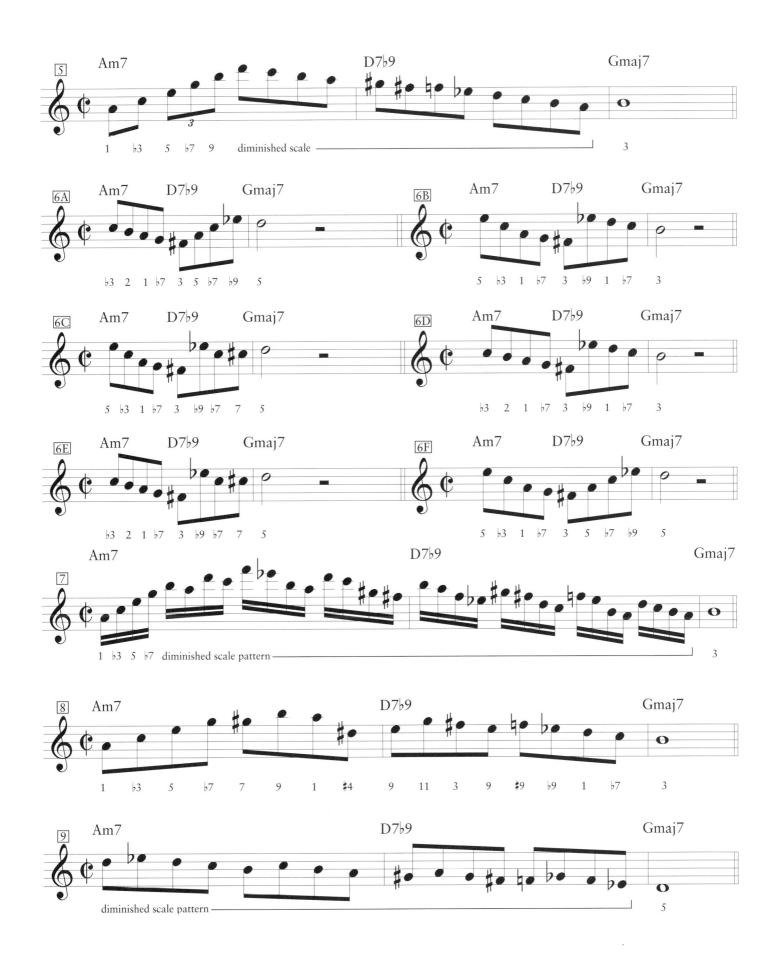

SAMUEL FURNACE

Sam Furnace plays all the saxophones, flute, clarinet, and is a composer and arranger. He has performed with Jaki Byard, Art Blakey, Abdullah Ibrahim, McCoy Tyner, Randy Weston, Al Hibbler, Tito Puente, Machito, Charli Persip, Chico O'Farrill, and Bernard Purdie. Mr. Furnace can be heard on recordings from Mongo Santamaria, Milt Hinton, Craig Harris, Fred Ho, Johnny Copeland, Elliot Sharp, the Julius Hemphill Saxophone Sextet, the New York Jazz Composers Orchestra, and the Jazz Passengers.

I use these exercises for warming up. They are also good for working on intonation when played slowly.

Two minor 7th intervals played a tritone apart create a dominant seventh chord with a flatted fifth.

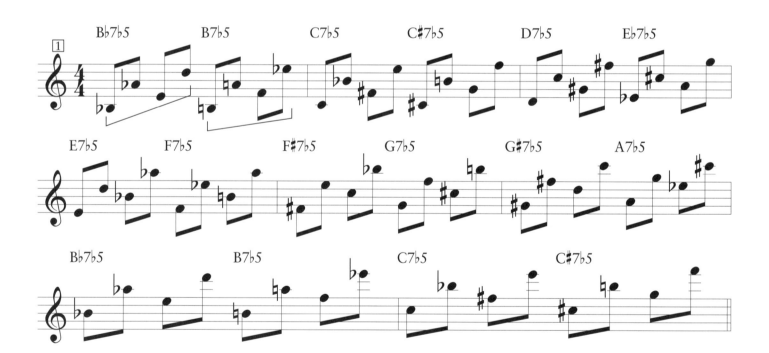

Two perfect 4ths played a major 3rd apart create a major seventh chord.

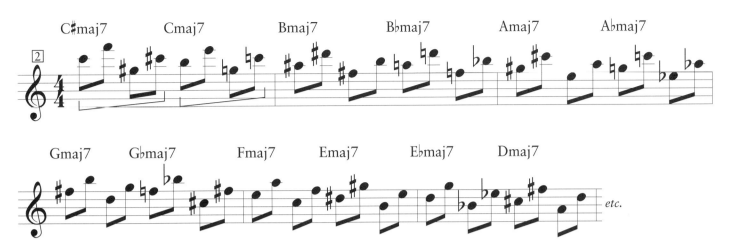

Same as pattern 2, with chords in different inversions.

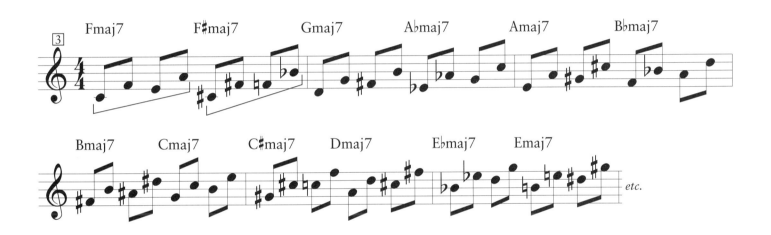

There are several relationships going on simultaneously:
1. The first and third beats of each bar outline a Cmaj9#11 chord.
2. Every other four-note grouping creates major chords played in the circle of 5ths.
3. Each four-note grouping is a major seventh chord, and the chords ascend by alternating major 3rds and minor 3rds.

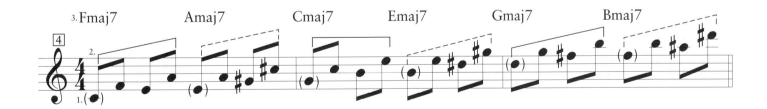

DAVE GLASSER

Dave Glasser is a regular member of the Clark Terry Quintet and has performed extensively with Illinois Jacquet, Barry Harris, and the Count Basie Orchestra under the direction of Frank Foster. In addition he has performed in concert with Dizzy Gillespie, Sir Roland Hanna, Sarah Vaughan, Billy Eckstine, Junior Mance, and many others. He has recorded with George Benson, Monty Alexander, Jaki Byard, and James Williams, among others, and his two CDs as a leader are Uh Oh *and* Dreams Askew, Dreams Anew. *Mr. Glasser teaches Bebop Harmony and Applied Saxophone at the New School in New York.*

This exercise, if attended to in detail, will insure the proper production of sound and articulation. The purpose is to develop a clean, clear beginning and ending to each note (no "fuu-fuu" attacks). This will insure a precise articulation of rhythm in your playing. Think of yourself as a drum: the clearer you are in articulating your rhythm, the easier it will be for others to play with you. A clean, clear staccato of sixteenth notes at quarter-note=120 can be achieved with patient, relaxed, and consistent effort.

1. With a relaxed jaw and oral cavity (throat) place the tip of the tongue on the tip of the reed so that no air can pass through the mouthpiece.
2. Take a breath, then set the air pressure with the diaphragm (keep upper body relaxed).
3. Release tongue (pull back off reed) to allow air to flow through the mouthpiece. This should produce a clean beginning to the note (think TUUU). Keep everything but the diaphragm calm and relaxed.
4. Place the tongue back on the reed to stop the note. This should produce a clean and precise ending to the note.
5. Keep diaphragm pressure constant while repeating steps 1 through 4 several times.
6. When almost out of breath, place the tongue on the reed to stop it vibrating, relax diaphragm pressure, and then release the tongue.
7. Increase speed of tonguing gradually, using proper technique, with clarity and quality of sound your priority.

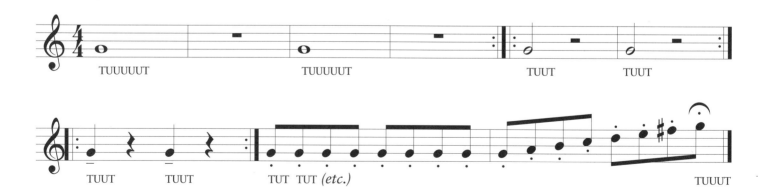

MARK GROSS

Mark Gross has toured the world with the Duke Ellington Orchestra conducted by Mercer Ellington and Paul Mercer Ellington. In addition to TV, film, and theater work, he has played in the bands of Tom Harrell, Philip Harper, and Nat Adderley. Mr. Gross has recorded with Antonio Hart, Delfeayo Marsalis, Masahiko Osaka, Gene Gardener, Ted Curson, Yoichi Kobayashi, Shingo Okudaira, and the Spirit of Life Ensemble. His recordings as a leader are Preach Daddy, Riddle of the Sphinx, *and* The Gospel According to Mark.

These examples show how a given pattern can be altered rhythmically to create a different melodic flow. By changing the rhythm of the notes in your melodic idea, you can come up with an infinite number of figures, all based on your initial idea. Practice these examples, then apply this concept to your own melodic patterns.

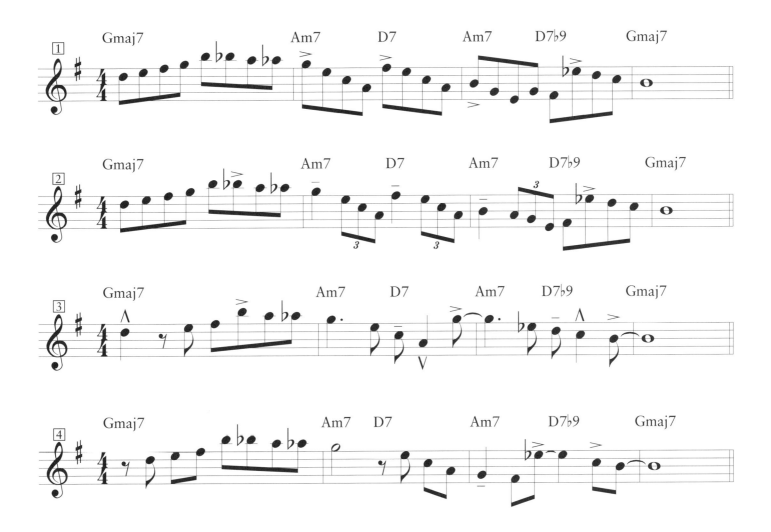

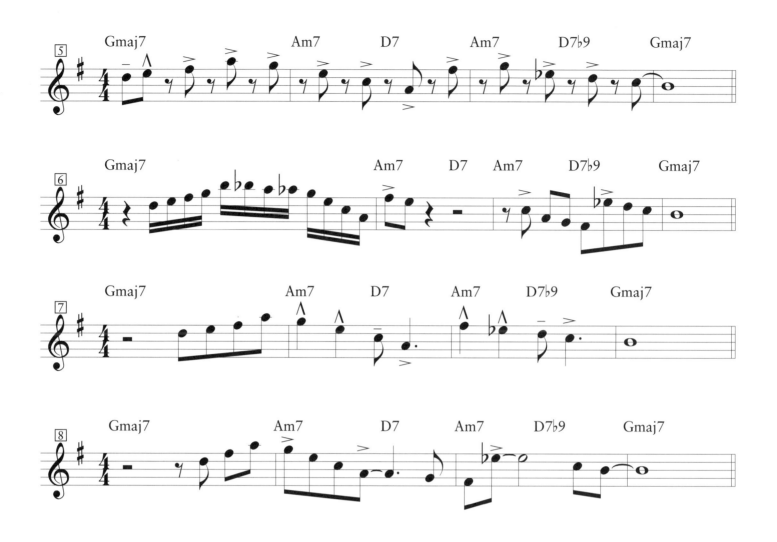

CLEAVE GUYTON

Cleave Guyton plays all the saxophones in addition to flute and clarinet. He has worked with Joe Henderson, Stanley Turrentine, Nat Adderley, Abbey Lincoln, the Ray Charles Orchestra, Spike Lee, Joe Williams, Dizzy Gillespie, Tito Puente, the Mingus Big Band, Cleo Laine, John Dankworth, the Count Basie Orchestra, Abdullah Ibrahim, and the Spirit of Life Ensemble, with whom he has recorded five CDs. Mr. Guyton has also recorded with Al Grey, George Gee, Greg Osby, the New York Composers Orchestra, and the Rhythm Team. He is currently the Music Director and lead alto of the Lionel Hampton Orchestra, with whom he recorded the 90th Birthday Celebration album.

This exercise is great for technique and flexibility in all keys. It's also great for learning the diatonic modes needed for playing jazz. It should be practiced daily, very slowly and evenly, starting with the metronome at 60. The tempo should gradually be increased over time to 120. The most important thing about this exercise is that it should be practiced in all keys, moving both through the circle of fifths and chromatically.

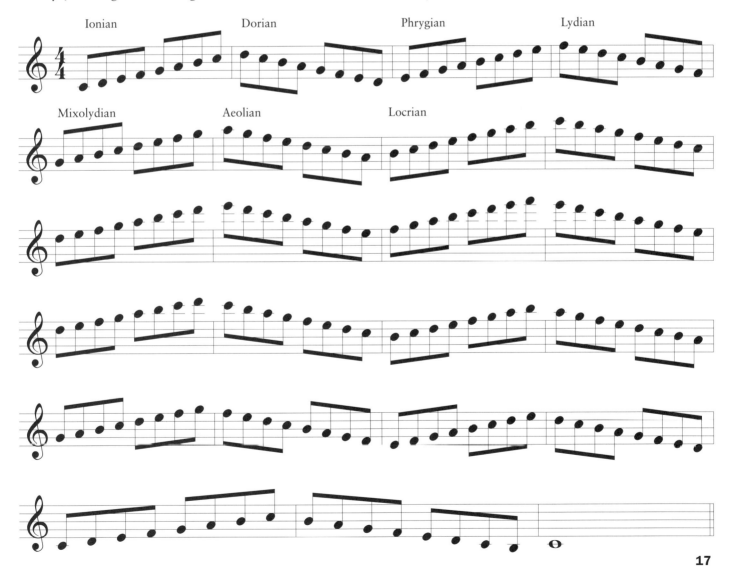

JENNY HILL

Jenny Hill is a New York-based saxophonist and flautist whose debut recording is titled Liquid Horn. *She has worked with jazz artists Clark Terry, Dave Brubeck, Joe Williams, Cab Calloway,* DIVA, *and with pop and world beat artists such as Maxi Priest, Burning Spear, Dennis Brown, Daniel Ponce, and MC Solar. Ms. Hill is a winner of the* JAZZIZ *magazine "Woodwinds on Fire" contest, and she is featured in the book* Rock and Roll Saxophone *by John Laughter.*

The study of tone production is something that is often neglected in younger saxophonists. After doing numerous big band clinics in high schools and colleges around the country, my colleagues and I noticed that the young brass players had full rich tones, while the young sax players often had thin, underdeveloped tones. We concluded that the brass players were products of a long history of classical tone production exercises passed on by their teachers, while the saxophone, being a relatively new instrument, did not yet have an accepted path to consistent quality tone production. Of course, a part of the tone quality is related to getting the proper set-up (mouthpiece, reed, ligature) for each individual. Your private teacher should be able to help you with the right choices.

At the beginning of my practice sessions, I do the Carmine Caruso longtone exercises for brass in all intervals from 2nds to 7ths. As I play each note, I work on speeding up the flow of air into the horn, while maintaining a firm embouchure, and keeping an eye on my tuner as well. I also listen to the overall quality of my tone, and strive to hear the rich overtone series inside of each note. After five to ten minutes of longtones, I move on to whichever scales or patterns I am concentrating on that day and play them in all octaves and through the range of the horn. Beginning your practicing with this sequence accomplishes several things:

- Mental and physical warming-up
- Focusing on sound before anything else
- Getting a lot of air to flow quickly through the horn
- Proper interval relationships
- Overall evenness and richness of tone throughout the entire range of the saxophone

Remember, what's the first thing you hear when someone starts soloing? How do you recognize the greats ('Trane, Sonny, Bird, Miles) immediately? Their sound! They all have unique, rich, and interesting tones.

Carmine Caruso exercise: Written using 2nds here, also do it in 3rds, 4ths, 5ths, 6ths, and 7ths from G to G, using all naturals. Watch your tuning, especially in the decrescendo at the end of each section. Support with your diaphragm. Listen, and work on the richness of your tone.

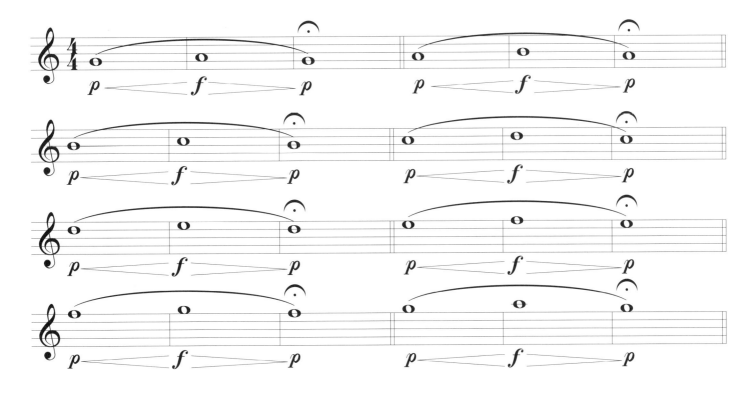

Example of a II V practiced in full range. Do two sets—each descending in whole steps. (The other set would begin on B♭m7 and end on Em7.) Strive for evenness of tone while moving through the pattern.

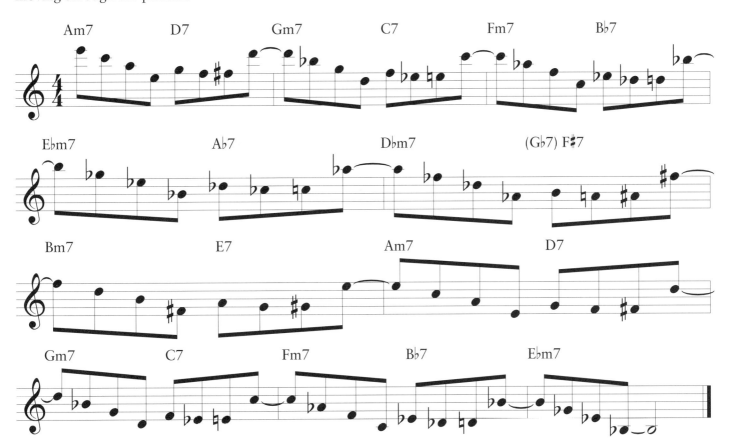

Practice at all tempos with the metronome on beats 2 and 4. Your goal is to feel limber and flexible throughout the range of the horn. You can create your own licks—just make sure you use the full range of the horn within each grouping. Listen to your tone—make sure the D's and E's aren't stuffy, and everything is in tune! Also vary the dynamic markings; even at *pianissimo*, your airstream should be moving quickly through the horn.

MARTHA HYDE

Martha Hyde is a multiple woodwind player who specializes in shows and projects in which jazz and European classical styles intersect. As a commercial player, she is often seen in Broadway pit orchestras, appearing on several cast albums such as Kiss of the Spiderwoman *with Vanessa Williams. She recorded incidental music for the Broadway play* Ride Down Mount Morgan *with Patrick Stewart, as well as several television jingles. Ms. Hyde has worked with a wide variety of entertainers, including Whoopi Goldberg, Bernadette Peters, Paul Sorvino, and Dizzy Gillespie.*

This exercise was inspired by Barry Harris, who used to have the students in his classes practice chains of major arpeggios moving by half steps. I tried relating them by whole steps (1) and then by minor thirds (2), and I liked them both. You can expand the exercise by making the starting note of each arpeggio the 3rd or the 5th, instead of the tonic.

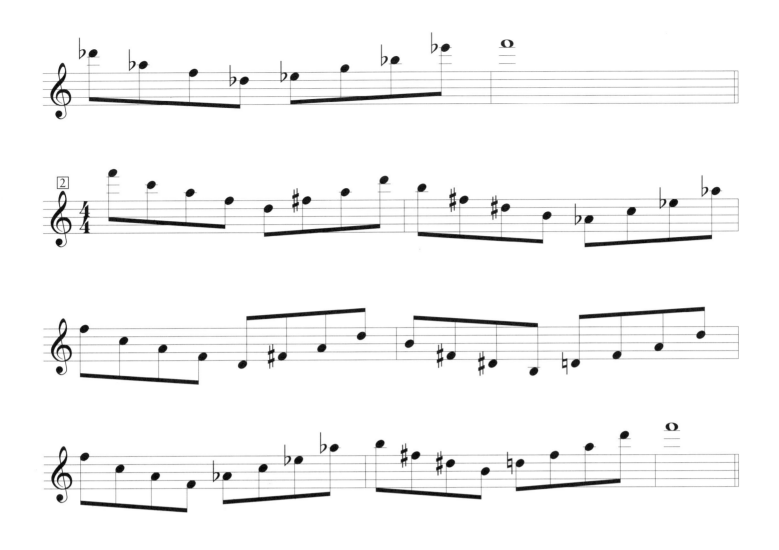

VIRGINIA MAYHEW

Virginia Mayhew arrived in New York from San Francisco in 1987. She has worked with Norman Simmons, Toshiko Akiyoshi, Lew Tabakin, Slide Hampton, Joe Williams, Leon Parker, Dottie Dodgion, Dena DeRose, Clark Terry, Terry Gibbs, Kenny Barron, Larry Goldings, and Brad Mehldau. Her tenure with veteran trombonist Al Grey is documented on his 1995 CD Centerpiece *(Telarc), and she has recorded with Sahib Shihab,* DIVA, *and the Jazz Nativity* Bending Towards the Light. *Ms. Mayhew's recordings as a leader are* Nini Green *(Chiaroscuro) and* No Walls *(Foxhaven).*

The purpose of this exercise is to get your fingers moving. Keep repeating the first bar until you get it as fast as possible. Then go on to the second bar, and so on. When you take a breath, go back to the beginning of the exercise, repeating each bar again until it is perfectly smooth. Toward the end of the exercise, you don't need to go back to the beginning after each breath. Use on all scales.

ANDY MIDDLETON

Andy Middleton is a New York City saxophonist/composer who has recorded four CDs as a leader: Reinventing the World *(Intuition),* Nomad's Notebook *(Intuition)* Terra Infirma *(Owl/EMI France)* Acid Rain *(Owl) as well as a play-along CD of his original compositions in the August 2000* Jazz Player *magazine, and a "Master Class" CD for* Saxophone Journal. *He recorded two CDs as a member of the Fensters, and has toured Europe as a leader and a sideman more than thirty times. Mr. Middleton has also performed and/or recorded with Lionel Hampton, Randy Brecker, John Abercrombie, Bob Mintzer, Adam Nussbaum, Maria Schneider, Marc Copeland, Barbara Dennerlein, and Danny Gottlieb, among others.*

To use the four-way interval system, practice any consistent group of notes (like 3rds on a major scale) in all four of its vertical permutations.

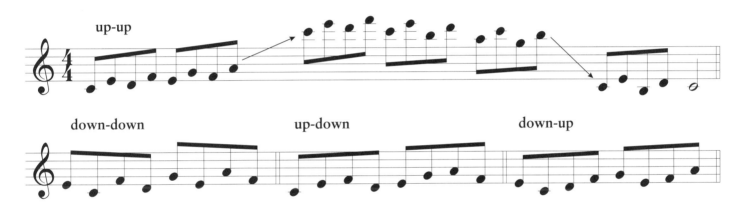

Now create a three-note group by stacking two intervals. For example, stack a major 2nd and a perfect 4th: C to D and D to G. Practice this note group using the four-way interval system described above, moving by half steps.

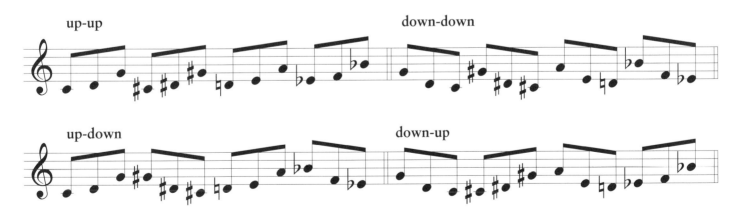

23

A more complex example of a three-note group is to stack a minor 3rd and a minor 6th: C to E♭ and E♭ (D♯) to B.

Create a four-note group by separating your two intervals by another interval. For example, a major 3rd and a minor 3rd separated by a major 3rd. This makes a major seventh chord with an augmented 5th: C to E and G♯ to B.

A more complex example of a four-note group is to stack two major-3rd intervals separated by a perfect 5th: C to E and B to D♯.

Practice your note groups using the four-way interval system moving by half steps, whole steps, minor 3rds, major 3rds, 4ths, and tritones, and you will have created a vast number of permutations on your note group which you can apply in your improvisations and compositions.

TOM MURRAY

Tom Murray is a New York City saxophonist, clarinetist, and flutist. He has played in the bands of Woody Herman, Brother Jack McDuff, and Walter Bishop, Jr. He has recorded with Jaki Byard and the Apollo Stompers, as well as the swing band the Flipped Fedoras. Mr. Murray has played in numerous Broadway shows both on Broadway and in international touring companies, including Fosse; Cats; Kiss Me, Kate; The Music Man; Victor/Victoria; *and* Annie Get Your Gun.

The blues scale is perhaps the most versatile scale in jazz, blues, and pop/rock/funk. It works best over dominant and minor chords, and to me it is most astounding because you can start on any note in the scale, on any beat in the measure, and it sounds great. Try different rhythmic figures, and experiment with different starting notes as pick-ups, triplets, down beats, mordents—anything! Like any exercise, this should be played in all keys throughout the range of the horn.

TOM OLIN

Tom Olin is a freelance saxophonist, clarinetist, and flutist residing in Brooklyn, New York. He has worked in the bands of Illinois Jacquet, Lionel Hampton, Gladys Knight, Eartha Kitt, Frank Foster, Jaki Byard, and Leonard Gaskin, as well as in many Broadway shows and Dixieland bands. Mr. Olin can be heard on recordings with the Bross Townsend Small Group, Bill Warfield Big Band, Sam Ulano, and Andy Jaffe.

This exercise strengthens your mind, your sound, and your ear, while getting you around the horn. The notes can be played in any rhythm. Do it in all keys.

JAY RODRIGUEZ

Jay Rodriguez plays all the saxophones, flute, and bass clarinet, as well as being a composer, arranger, and producer. Born in Colombia, South America, he moved to New York with his family in 1971. Mr. Rodriguez has worked in the bands of Tito Puente, Chucho Valdes, Elvin Jones, the Mingus Big Band, and Jon Faddis. He has worked and recorded with Prince, Wu-Tang Clan, Live Tropical Fish, Sha-Key, Cibo Matto, Medeski Martin & Wood, Groove Collective, Giant Step, Organized Confusion, Meir Ben Michael, Eightball, Ray Barretto, Bobby Sanabria, A.V., Clark Gayton, Eric Gadd, Victor Jones, Jazzy Nice, Annie Lennox, Roy Nathanson, Elvis Costello, Bill Ware, Guru, Josh Roseman, Batidos, Eddie Bobe, the Bellwether Project, Orimar's Flying Machine, and Amber Sunshower.

As saxophone artists, we sometimes have to interpret a sonic language that we do not yet hear or know how to pronounce. In order to be comfortable in the dimension of music, our ear (and mind) must be willing to accept all possible intervals and melodic settings. This etude was developed with that in mind. Suggestions: Find your interpretation, your sound—your personal voice on your instrument. Play the etude *rubato*, repeat measures and sections, transpose them if you like, concentrating on sound and dynamics. Be patient with intervals you may not be accustomed to.

BENNY RUSSELL

Benny Russell began his career while still a student at Morgan State University. He plays tenor, alto, and soprano saxophones in addition to flute, clarinet, and bass clarinet. He has worked with Otis Rush, Harry Belafonte, Mino Cinelu, Craig Harris, Jimmy Owens, Junior Cook, Abdullah Ibrahim, Mor Thium, the Manhattans, the Four Tops, Richard "Groove" Holmes, and David Murray—and he was the founder of the jazz orchestra New York Association. He has played on numerous movie and TV soundtracks, including The Cosby Show. *Mr. Russell co-leads the nineteen-piece Next Legacy Orchestra, and he is head of the jazz department at the Brooklyn Conservatory of Music. His own recording,* Proverbs, *is on Airmen Records.*

This is a cycle that moves in 4ths. Much of Western music moves this way, so it is important not only to outline the chord in an argpeggiated fashion to understand its components, but also to train the ear to hear that kind of movement. When you practice, you exercise not just the fingers and embouchure, but the ear as well.

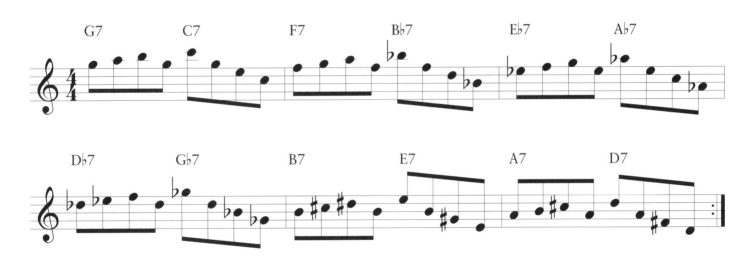

This is a cycle that moves in tritones. When working on tritone substitutions, it is helpful to spell out the chords. This exercise covers all the inversions of the chords (here C major and F♯ major) and should be done in all keys.

ANDREW STERMAN

Andrew Sterman is a member of the Philip Glass Ensemble, with which he travels extensively and has recorded eleven CDs and three film scores, including Kundun *and* The Truman Show. *He lives in New York City, where he has developed and teaches a system of flute, saxophone and clarinet playing that incorporates elements of* Taiji *and* QiGong, *the ancient arts of healing with breath and movement, in which he is a certified teacher. Mr. Sterman has played with Freddie Hubbard, Rashied Ali, Fred Hersch, Frank Sinatra, Dizzy Gillespie, Sarah Vaughan, Buddy Rich, Wallace Roney, and Aretha Franklin—and he is very active on Broadway, in freelance recording, and in a wide variety of classical and improvising ensembles.*

The Looping Breath

Although we play the saxophone with our exhalation, the quality of our sound is controlled by the way we inhale. Once the air is inside our bodies, it is too late to drop tensions or increase our resonance. So a good inhalation exercise is important.

Good breathing involves more unlearning than learning. At all levels of playing, we can discover tensions in our breathing, and it's essential to find ways to release these tensions before adding any more effort. Breathing should be natural and unaffected, allowing our sound to flow freely and with personality, fully integrated with time feel, phrasing, intonation, and melodic invention. The *looping breath* is one way to deepen and free our breath without adding the sound of effort to our playing. Begin by practicing the breath without your instrument.

Basic Looping Breath

1. Inhale about half a full breath,
2. Exhale a small amount of air, and
3. Inhale the remainder of a full breath.

The middle exhalation is the Loop. Everything should be round and your breath should never come to a stop.

Exploring the looping breath is a very effective way to improve your sound, as it releases tensions and increases efficiency. At first you should practice slowly; gradually it will be easy to do a quick looping breath without any effort. Eventually, for very quick breaths, you will find that you can attain the feeling of a good looping breath without the loop at all.

More Detail

Let's look in more detail at the looping breath. Without going stiff, gently adjust your posture so that you are not slouching forward, nor leaning to the left or right. Let your shoulders down and soften your lower back. At first, this is best done standing. Gently take in a medium breath, exhale just a little, then breathe in some more. Have a sense of ease throughout. Sometimes even fine players have a moment in their breathing where there is a stop before the breath changes direction, from in to out or out to in. I call this a *corner*—it stiffens the flow of air and disconnects the air in your torso from the air in your mouth. Try again and make a round change of air direction; hold in your mind the image of rounding out the corners. Breathe in a half breath, round the corner, breathe out just a little, round the corner, breathe in another half breath or a little more. And of course, round the corner after the completed breath, to begin the exhalation which blows the note.

At this point, ask yourself a question or two. Can you hear air rushing past the back of your tongue? This is a sign of tension and air obstruction, causing turbulence. Just before beginning the breath, try to relax any part of the breath pathway which could cause noise. (You might begin by relaxing the lips and tongue and then continue in and down toward the larynx, ribs, belly, and lower back. If you can relax from your embouchure to your heels while playing, then you've really got it!) A second question to explore is whether the muscles between your ribs are stiff. If they are, this will inhibit your breathing, slowing it down and giving it unnecessary resistance. It's like trying to inflate a balloon while someone is holding it tight, trying to prevent it expanding. There used to be a popular exercise fad called isometrics, where bulky muscles were developed by pressing your own arms against each other, but this pressing against your own muscles is a terrible way to breathe! It is very important to release the muscles of your own balloon before the breath begins.

Return to your looping breath. This time, release these holding muscles in your ribs or belly, breathe in the first part, exhale the small loop while releasing any more holding, inhale the second part, all while maintaining rounded breath corners. Apply this breath to your instrument. Although this exercise is not complicated, it is natural for tension to creep in as our tasks get more layered: breathing, then breathing and playing, then breathing and playing something difficult, then breathing while playing with others or in performance. At each point, mentally return to the effortless function that you have established so easily while practicing the looping breath, dropping any holding tension, and allowing your breath to flow in, around and out as the physical foundation for the flow of your sound. With the image of the loop, the breathing should easily be tension-free and deep, providing a surprisingly strong, colorful, and effortless tone.

Advanced Practice
As you advance with this technique, use your imagination to explore new aspects. For example, imagine that there is a kind of board or plank just below the mid-line of your torso. Imagine it extending from one side of your torso to the other, and from front to back; be very simple with this and call it a rectangular board. Imagine this board to be laying flat beneath your ribs, at the floor of the lungs, like the physical diaphragm, but not as complicated in its movement or anatomical features. As you breathe in, the board sinks down; with the loop it rises slightly while staying basically flat. With the second inhalation it drops down more. As you play a note or phrase the board rises, wide and even. Gradually expand the sides of the board, so that the breath scrubs the inside walls of your torso. This feeling of wide breathing can be expanded far past the physical limits of your body itself. Explore the results when the board remains truly even side to side, or as you imagine it tipping to the back as you inhale (which is what the diaphragm itself does).

Imagining a wide board in the location of your diaphragm can be very helpful in sensing and improving how your belly is working with breath. This is the lower half of good breathing. The upper half is, generally speaking, your ribs, neck, and head. To explore this, an advanced player may wish to turn the breathing around.

Imagine that the breath loops up your back as you inhale, forward and down as you let go the very small loop, and again up your back as you inhale the second. This will feel as if you are breathing up your spine, looping, and again breathing up the spine to the back of your head, around over the top, and down past your nose. The blowing of the horn feels like the breath descending. As you get comfortable with this, all aspects of the breathing feel like loops. To feel this more easily, try tracing an image of the breath in front of you. With your hands together in front of your torso, gently move them in and up as you are inhaling the first inhalation; your hands come in slightly toward your shirt buttons and up the center line; as you let go the small loop your hands loop forward just a little and down; as you continue with the second inhalation your hands come back in toward your buttons and loop up toward your nose, where they loop forward and down, which shows the blowing of the notes. Let your ribs and shoulders move with the breath, which causes no trouble as long as they float up and down on top of the breath with no holding. The hand movements should be smooth and linear, with no tension or sharp corners. This can be very helpful in understanding how to breathe without those corners which are really moments when the breathing stops and gets rigid.

Combining these two advanced exercises, you can feel two aspects simultaneously: First, something square or rectangular in the lower part of the torso, represented by the board, which sinks down with breathing in and rises up as you play or exhale. Second, something round, represented by your hands showing the arc of breath ascending up your back, around and up under your nose as it comes forward and down as blowing. These two aspects of breathing are complementary and truly can happen at once, as a fully integrated way of breathing and playing. As with the basic looping breath, with experience this comes to feel as natural as it really is, and the benefits are yours whether you take a careful looping breath or just a quick breath with the feeling of loose fullness that you have become accustomed to through the exercises.

TAIMUR SULLIVAN

Taimur Sullivan has performed throughout Europe, Latin America, and the U.S. as a solo artist and with his saxophone quartet, PRISM. *He made his Carnegie Hall debut as a soloist with the National Wind Ensemble, and has also performed with the Detroit Symphony, Dallas Symphony, and* Nouvel Ensemble Moderne. *Active in commissioning new repertoire for the saxophone, he has given the premieres of over forty works by both established and emerging composers. Mr. Sullivan has recorded for the Mode, Innova, Capstone, Mastersounds, Zuma, and Bonk record labels, and regularly performs with many of New York's classical and contemporary music ensembles. He currently serves on the performance faculty of Columbia University.*

An Introduction to Overtones

Practicing overtones is an invaluable exercise for saxophonists performing in any genre of music to incorporate into their daily warm-ups. The exercises, whereby fingering the lowest notes *(fundamentals)* on the saxophone one is able to obtain higher notes *(harmonics* or *overtones)* by slight changes in the throat and oral cavity, are helpful in at least two important ways. First, by finding the throat's 'voicing' where the harmonics respond, the player will obtain a richer, more vibrant sound throughout the instrument. Second, by increasing awareness of the oral cavity's role, one will also have a better control of, and tone in, the altissimo range.

The overtone series is based on a pattern of gradually decreasing intervals as the harmonics ascend. The first three octaves look like this.

(Note: For the purposes of this exercise, all examples are given using the harmonic series based on the low B♭. However, in daily practice they should be transposed to include low B, C, and C♯ as the fundamentals.)

Eventually, you will be able to produce each of these pitches while fingering low B♭. However, this is not an easy task, so to begin the practice of overtones, we will start with the goal of producing one-octave overtones—in this case a sounding middle B♭, while fingering a low B♭. You may find that, by slightly narrowing the oral cavity or raising the back of your tongue, you can achieve this without much difficulty. It may be helpful to add the octave key momentarily, to help the overtone speak. Or you may find that while the first octave harmonic is difficult to produce, the octave-and-a-fifth harmonic pops out more easily. The following progression of fingerings may provide a more gradual "trick" to this first harmonic, as it gradually closes toneholes from a common "one-and-one" B♭ fingering until the overtone fingering is reached.

Some notes to keep in mind while practicing this and other overtone exercises:

- Keep the airstream focused and fast.
- Experiment with both "h" and "k" attack—either "hee" and "huh" or "kee" and "kuh."
- Try not to use a standard tongue articulation, as this can cause tension in the early stages of developing overtone technique.
- Be aware of your throat position. Often, moving to an "ee" syllable in the throat is helpful in obtaining ascending harmonics, while gradually opening to an "oo" syllable can be helpful when descending.
- Don't bite harder, or get tense in the mouth and throat! The purpose of these exercises is to promote flexibility throughout the instrument while maintaining a comfortable and consistent embouchure and throat position.

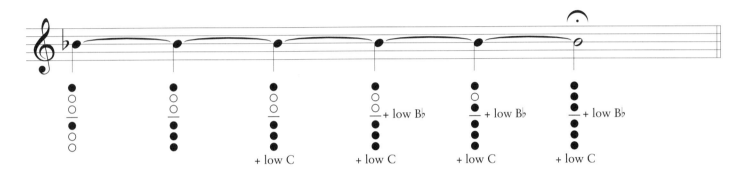

Then, practice moving chromatically on the one-octave harmonic. *(Note: In these examples, the lower pitches represent the note to finger, while the upper notes show the pitch that should be sounding.)*

A similar approach will help in producing the octave-and-a-fifth harmonic.

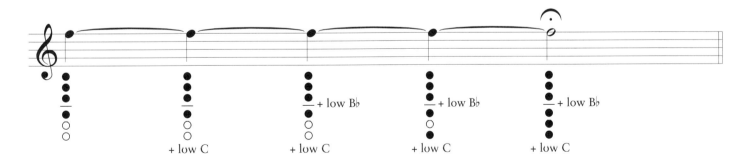

You can extend this concept to include higher harmonics as well. Then, practice smoothly slurring between a regular note and its corresponding overtone fingering (and use a tuner to make sure the overtones, as well as the regular notes, stay in tune!).

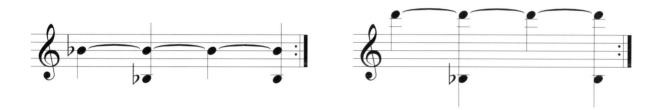

With daily practice, you will eventually find yourself able to play through the three octave harmonic series notated above, and even higher. Finally, use your newly developed skills to play familiar tunes, such as the bugle call "Reveille." Play this while fingering only a low B♭ throughout.

Please let this serve only as an introduction to a larger world of overtone practice; as you develop, create your own exercises and routines that challenge and extend your abilities with this technique.

JORGE SYLVESTER

Jorge Sylvester was born in Colon, Panama, where he attended the Panama Conservatory of Music. He relocated first to Madrid, Spain, and then to the U.S., studying at the Creative Music Studio in Woodstock, New York, and graduating from New Paltz University in 1981. He is the co-leader of the nineteen-piece Next Legacy Orchestra and a member of the saxophone quartet Collective Identity. Mr. Sylvester has also recorded with Devorah Day and Marion Brown, Sekou Sundiata, the Essence All Stars, Miguel Angel Chastang, and the group Batimco, in which he is the featured composer. He co-led the recording Magic Night *on Jazz Stop with Miguel Chastang, and his recordings as a leader include* Musicollage *(Postcard) and* In the Ear of the Beholder *(Jazz Magnet). He teaches at the Brooklyn Conservatory of Music in New York City.*

This study is to be played for ear training purposes. To accustom your ear to these intervals, the study should be played as many times as possible. The intervals are not designed for any specific chord, you can use them as you like when you begin to hear them naturally. Vary the exercise by changing the rhythm or switching the octaves around.

SUE TERRY

Every tone you play has many parts, or levels, to it. The most obvious part, the one that stands out to the ear as we play, is the part that contains the sound of the airstream itself. This part has an "edge" to it; you can hear the upper partials, or "treble" part of the sound, very clearly. Many players never get beyond listening only to this part of the sound.

Behind this sound is what I call the *shadow tone*. This part of the tone has no upper partials. It sounds very much like a sine wave tone produced on a synthesizer. It is not affected by vibrato; it remains a pure tone even while you're doing vibrato.

If you keep listening very intently to the sound as you play sustained tones, after a while you will begin to hear these two parts, or levels, of the sound quite clearly. The awareness of the shadow tone may fade in and out, and this is fine. By focusing on becoming aware of the shadow tone, you are stimulating the intensity and projection of your sound.

Although this exercise may be done on any wind instrument or with the voice, the shadow tone may be affected by certain characteristics of the type of instrument you're playing. For instance, on a saxophone, the airstream changes direction as it follows the curve of the instrument at the bottom of the bell. So if you play a note at this section of the horn, such as low E♭, you may hear that the shadow tone is of a different pitch than the main tone. It may differ by a half step, whole step, or more. This phenomenon may allow you to hear the shadow tone more clearly. Playing against a wall is also useful, because the sound bounces back at you.

After your ear is well practiced at "grabbing" the shadow tone, you can begin to focus on other parts of the sound, such as overtones. When I play longtones, I hear very distinctly several overtones at once. When I focus very intently on the overtones, sometimes they can begin to dominate the aural spectrum, so that the original tone actually disappears into the background.

One way to practice your longtones is to play them in a set interval within the diatonic scale. For instance, if I choose the interval of a 5th, I would start on low B♭, then up to F, then the next diatonic note of G, and down to C, then D, and up a 5th to A, and so on. When you get to the top, you can come down the same way, or you can come down on the next scale, the scale of B major. This exercise is also great for intonation.

After a few weeks of using the interval of a 5th, experiment with other intervals. You can also use scales other than the major scale. By varying your longtone practice in this way, you can sustain your interest in studying your tone. This exercise enables you to distill your sound so that to others, it becomes recognizable immediately as your personal sound. After all, despite all the cool runs and licks you may be able to play, the first thing heard is the quality of your tone.

ABOUT THE AUTHOR

Sue Terry is an alto and soprano saxophonist who began her professional career in Hartford, Connecticut, where she was a graduate of the Hartt School, and a protégé of saxophonist Jackie McLean. She also studied saxophone with Robert Kolb and Paul Jeffrey; clarinet with William Roos and Henry Larsen; flute with Hal Archer; composition with Edward Diemente; the Kodaly System with Janos Horvath; jazz with Jaki Byard, Walter Bishop, Jr., and Alexander Lepak; and piano and theory with John Mehegan. She settled in New York in 1982, where her mentors Barry Harris, Clifford Jordan, and Junior Cook dubbed her "Sweet Sue."

Ms. Terry has worked with Dr. Billy Taylor, Clark Terry, Al Jarreau, Walter Bishop, Jr., Chaka Khan, George Duke, Hilton Ruiz, Irene Reid, Juan Carlos Formell, Dr. John, Teri Thornton, Mike Longo, and Dianne Reeves, among others. She has appeared as a jazz soloist with the National Symphony, the Brooklyn Philharmonic, and the New York Pops conducted by Skitch Henderson.

Her compositions are featured on *The Troubadours* (Consolidated Artists) as co-leader of the group Terra Mars. Other artists whose recordings have featured her playing and writing include Charli Persip, Clifford Jordan, Joe McMahon, Derwyn Holder, Mini All Stars, Jaki Byard, Ricardo Franck, Fred Ho, and DIVA. She is Musical Director of the dance/music ensemble Beauteez 'N The Beat.

Widely known as an educator, she has conducted numerous clinics, workshops, and lectures throughout the U.S., and is a member of the International Association of Jazz Educators. A longtime practitioner of the ancient arts of *Taiji* and *QiGong,* she is a certified teacher of the Six Healing Sounds.

More about Ms. Terry's career can be found at www.sueterry.net, and in the book *Madame Jazz* by Leslie Gourse (her photograph appears on the book's cover).

Sue Terry is a Yamaha artist, and uses Consoli Ramplig ligatures.